A closer LOOK at ARCTIC LANDS

J. L. Hicks

Illustrated by
R. Coombs, D. Cordery, M. Wilson

Franklin Watts · New York · 1977

The Arctic world

We usually think of the Arctic—the area at the top of the world around the North Pole—as a frozen, lifeless place. But between the icy Arctic seas and the northern forests, there is a large area that is not just cold and empty. This is called the tundra, from an old word used by the Finns. The tundra stretches around the northern world in a belt. It covers five million square miles—a tenth of the land surface of the earth. While the climate of the tundra is cold and harsh, and there are almost no trees, it is a home for many plants and animals.

During the long winter, the North Pole leans away from the sun and the Arctic gets very little warmth. When summer comes, the heat is only strong enough to melt the snow cover and thaw the top layer of earth. Three feet or so below that, the ground stays frozen. This permanently frozen layer is called the permafrost.

The far north is very dry, as well as cold, and most of the tundra gets as little moisture (rain and snow) as a desert—less than ten inches a year. Without the permafrost, there wouldn't be enough water to support plant and animal life. This stone-hard layer stops the water from draining away into the earth. The soil above it freezes and thaws, but the moisture is held so the land can support life.

Land of the Midnight Sun

When the sun shines on the Arctic, it delivers much less heat and light than it does at the equator. The sun's rays hit polar areas at an angle, not directly. At the poles, the same amount of energy that is received at the equator is spread over a larger area.

The earth tilts to one side as it spins. For part of the year the North Pole leans toward the sun, and the days are very long. On June 21 the sun doesn't set anywhere north of the Arctic Circle. In winter, the North Pole leans away from the sun and Arctic days are short. On December 22 the sun never rises. The North Pole itself—the center of the Land of the Midnight Sun—has a six-month day (when the sun is always above the horizon) and a six-month night (when the sun never rises).

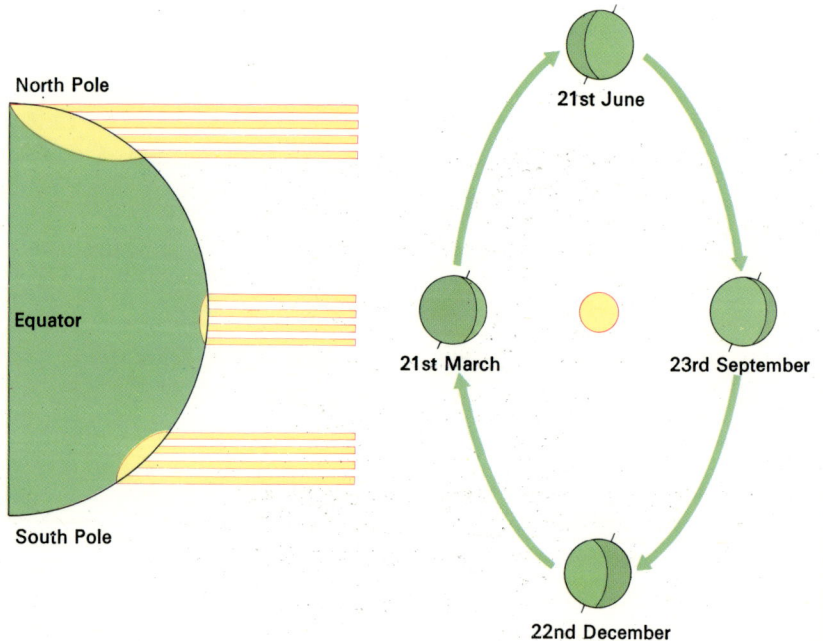

North Pole

Equator

South Pole

21st June

21st March

23rd September

22nd December

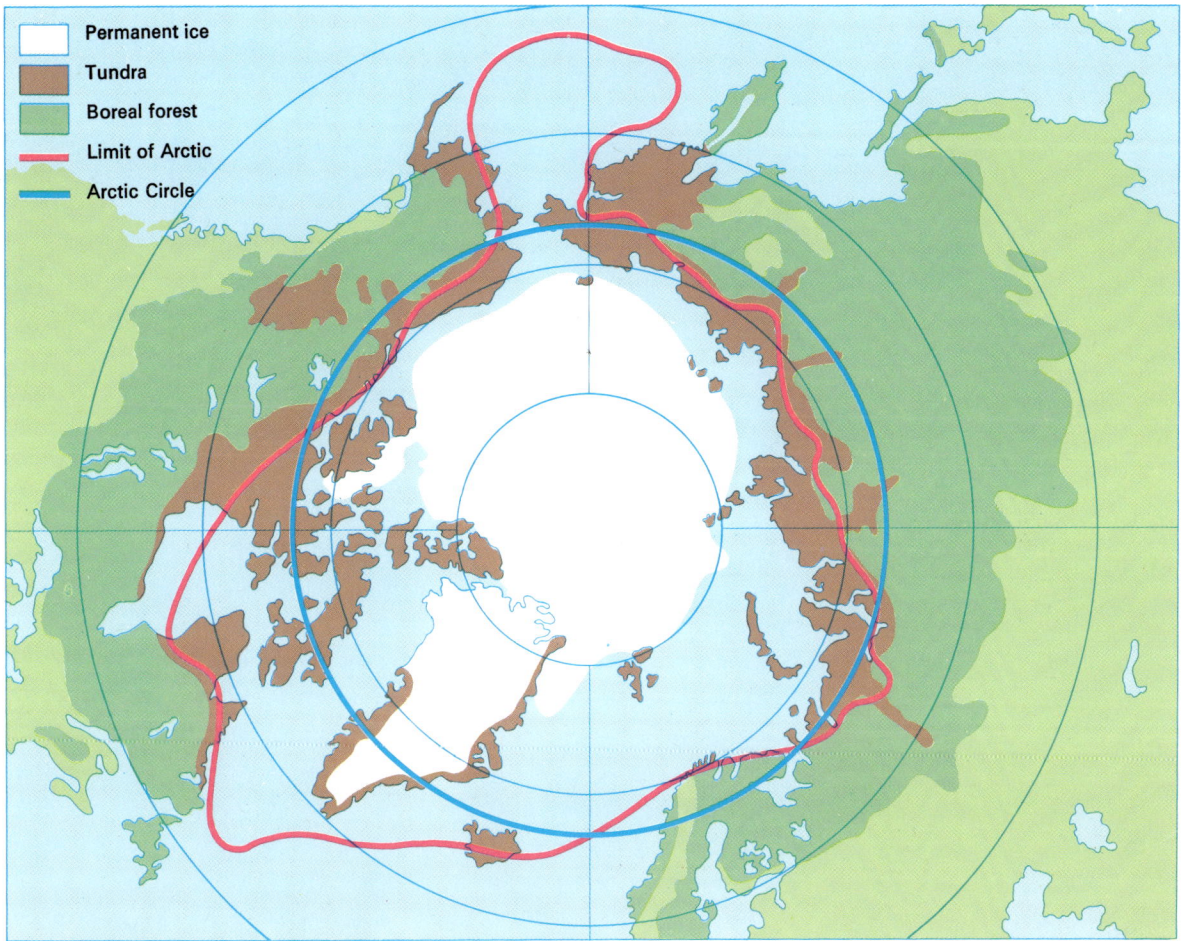

	Permanent ice
	Tundra
	Boreal forest
	Limit of Arctic
	Arctic Circle

The forest

The Arctic Circle, like the equator, is an imaginary line. A natural border to mark the Arctic is the tree line—the northern edge of the forest beyond which trees cannot grow. The tree line closely follows another natural boundary: a line called the 50° summer isotherm. North of this, the average summer temperature is below 50°.

The tundra

The tree line is a broad and fuzzy boundary; trees spread over the edge onto sheltered valleys of the tundra. There are areas of forest-tundra between the forest and the tundra. Some parts of the tundra are still developing; soil builds up after the ice sheets retreat.

Sea ice

At the northern edge of the land, the tundra meets the sea. Most of the Arctic Ocean is covered all year by sea ice, which might be twelve feet thick in winter. In summer, the ice sometimes breaks up and large stretches of water are exposed.

Shaping the land

The retreat of the ice

The earth is in the second half of the fourth ice age. Ice sheets (white areas) once spread over the northern half of the world. The ice cap (blue area) still covers much of the Arctic Ocean.

We live in an ice age. While our homes aren't threatened by the glaciers, or masses of moving ice, that covered much of Europe and North America 10,000 years ago, there are still huge sheets of ice covering the North Polar sea and many Arctic islands. Most of Greenland is covered by a thick ice cap.

In the northern half of the world, our ice age began about three million years ago, a short period in the earth's history. For 150 million years before that, Arctic lands were ice-free and had trees and warm-climate animals. Since then, great ice caps have formed, moved south, and retreated north again four times. The last thaw, or retreat, began 20,000 years ago; it is still going on. If the thaw continues long enough, the ice caps will melt and ocean levels will rise above low coastal areas.

The land of the far north

The ice cap has retreated to the mountainous land mass from which it came. The recently uncovered tundra appears to be more water than land because the permafrost keeps pools of water standing on the surface. The tundra is marked by strange features: pingos and eskers. Pingos are large broken-topped hills filled with ice. They might have once been lakes that dried up. The permafrost then pushed upward and formed a mound covered in thin soil. Eskers are long low ridges of silt and gravel that mark the beds of rivers that flowed under the ice sheets. When the ice retreated, deposits of silt and gravel were left—like abandoned railroad tracks. South of the tundra lies the northern, or boreal, forest.

When the ice sheets spread, they were like giant bulldozers that flattened the earth. Some species of plants and animals were cut off without a route to warmer areas and became extinct when the ice covered their living places.

When the ice sheets retreated north, they uncovered bare rock and gravel with no soil or life. Lichens and algae—forms of plant life that can survive on bare rock—are among the first living things that return to such land. They produce chemicals that break down the rock. A simple kind of soil is formed that can support mosses. Other plants and tiny animals follow. When they die, their bodies enrich the soil so it can support other life. This slow process continues until it produces the thin soil of the tundra. Now, after 10,000 years, the tundra has become land that can support many species of plants and animals.

Crazy paving

After freezing and thawing many times, the surface of low ground cracks and water fills the cracks. When the water freezes and expands, the cracks get larger, so more water can get in during the next thaw. The pressure of the water pushes the earth up on both sides of the cracks, forming basins that make patterns on the surface of the ground.

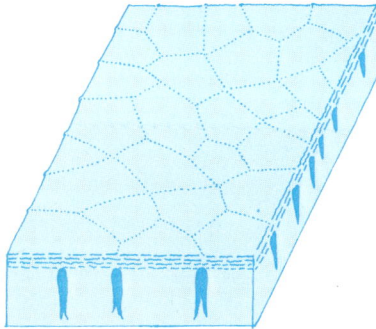

Glaciers

When snow builds up on mountains, it becomes packed into ice. The force of its own weight starts the ice moving downhill. Piles of rubble called moraines are carried down from the mountains by the advancing glaciers.

Mountains

Not all Arctic land is low. While many of the old mountain chains have been worn down by glaciers, there are still ranges that tower over the surrounding land and sea.

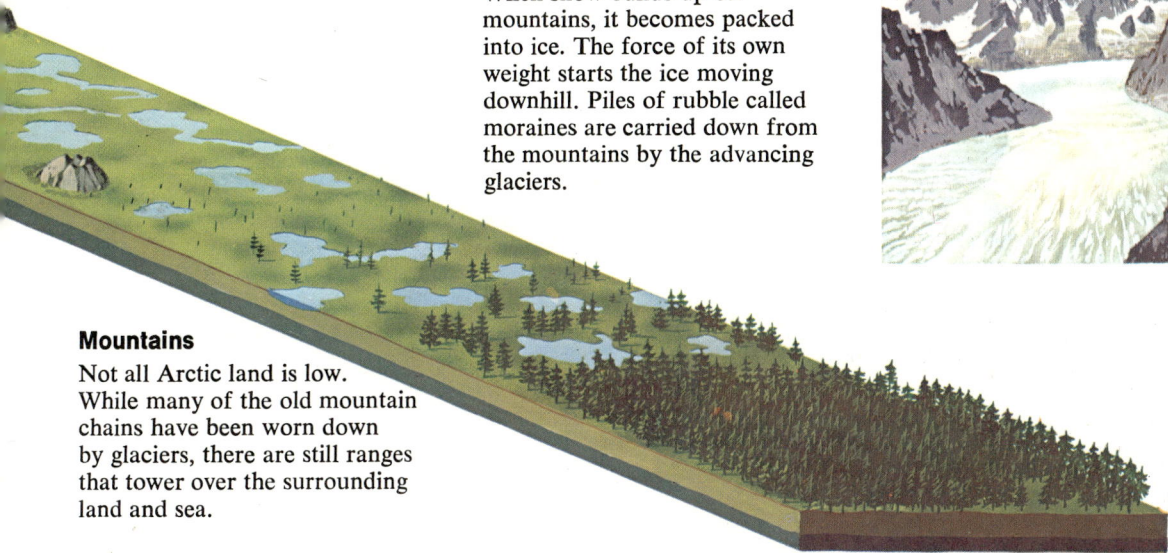

Tundra plants

It is hard for plants to survive on the tundra. The land is so poor that only a third of it can support plant life. Where the ground slopes, the top layer often loses its grip on the permafrost below and slips downhill, pulling up plant roots as it slides. The growing season may be as short as six weeks. Few plants have adapted to such hard conditions: there are about 2,500 kinds of lichens and mosses and about 900 species of flowers.

The species that survive have developed special ways to live. They grow close to the ground for warmth and protection from wind. The dwarf willow stretches branches ten feet over the surface but grows only four inches high. Some flowers, like the moss campion, grow in tight clumps to trap sunlight and warm air. The Arctic poppy even has "fur"— hair-like fibers on its leaves.

Reproduction is the biggest problem. Annuals—plants that live for only one year and must grow, flower, and drop seeds in one summer—seldom survive since a freeze can kill the whole species. Nearly all the plants are perennials that stretch their life cycles over several years. Buds may develop, freeze in the winter, and start growing again in the spring. If an early fall freeze stops seed production, the plant tries again the next year. Some plants don't reproduce by seeds. Shoots or buds grow out from the parent plant, break off, and take root themselves.

Saxifrages

Saxifrages reproduce by sending out long shoots with buds. These shoots then grow into new plants.

Lichens and mosses

A lichen is really two plants— a fungus and an alga—that live as partners. The fungus stores water and minerals, but since it has no chlorophyll, it can't convert sunlight into food. The alga produces food, which it shares with the fungus in return for water. Mosses are more advanced plants that can convert sunlight into food; they absorb water through their leaves.

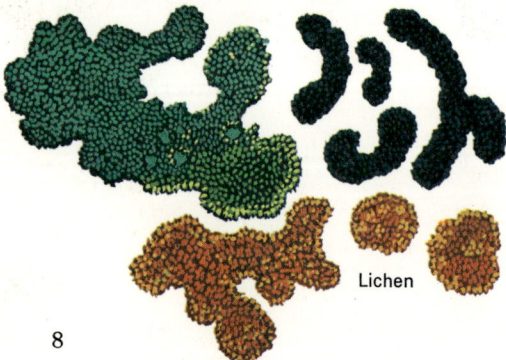

Moss

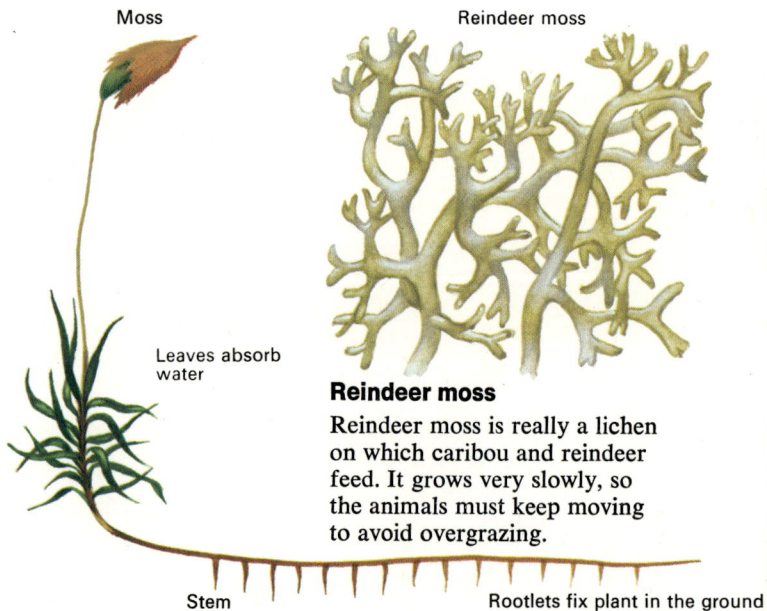

Reindeer moss

Leaves absorb water

Reindeer moss

Reindeer moss is really a lichen on which caribou and reindeer feed. It grows very slowly, so the animals must keep moving to avoid overgrazing.

Lichen

Stem

Rootlets fix plant in the ground

Insects

There are more species of insects than any other animal on the tundra. Every spring a new generation of insects is hatched.

Bumblebee

The large and furry bumblebee is the only species of bee to survive in the harsh Arctic.

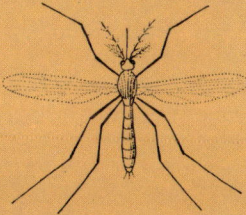

Mosquito

Mosquitoes thrive on the tundra. The small pools are like nurseries where the eggs hatch.

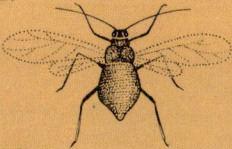

Blackfly

Like the mosquito, the small, biting blackfly develops in the tundra pools.

Butterfly

Arctic butterflies stay close to the ground to keep as warm as possible.

Flowering plants

Many flowering plants on the tundra are self-pollinating—the plant is fertilized by pollen produced on the same plant. Few plants depend only on seeds to survive. Berries are the safest way to spread seeds: Animals eat the berries; the seeds pass through their bodies and are deposited on the ground.

Mountain avens

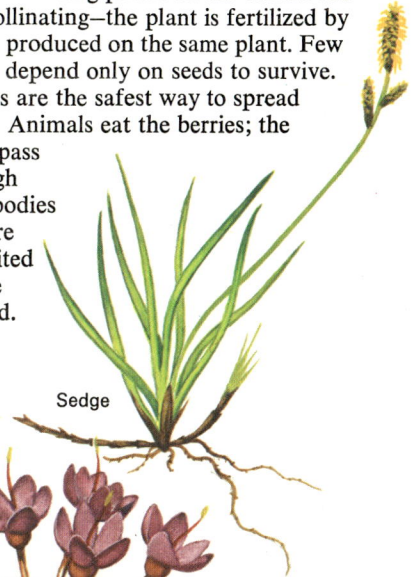

Sedge

Arctic poppy

Arctic rhododendron

Cloudberry

Arctic willow

Cranberry

Crowberry

Bilberry

Permanent residents

Very few of the higher animals—vertebrates, or animals with backbones—live on the tundra all year long. Many come for the summer, but only about a dozen species of mammals and a half dozen species of birds stay for the winter.

This small group of animals is linked by food chains—energy is passed from the sun to plants, from plants to animals. It is easy to see the chains or relationships on the tundra, since there are so few forms of life. Arctic plants are food for lemmings, mouse-like voles, and other herbivores, or plant eaters. These animals in turn are food for the carnivores, or meat eaters. Carnivores range from the powerful, intelligent wolf to the tiny shrew, which eats insects and grubs. The adventurous Arctic fox follows polar bears onto sea ice to get their leftovers. Ferocious weasels attack hares twenty-five times their weight. Owls and gyrfalcons prey on small mammals and other birds, and the raven eats just about anything—vegetable or animal, fresh or rotten.

One of the biggest tundra animals is the musk-ox, a herbivore that feeds on twigs and grass. These quiet creatures travel in small herds. When threatened, they form a circle around their young. The oxen face out, with heads lowered and horns ready. Unfortunately, this is no defense against rifles. Two hundred years ago, countless numbers of musk-oxen roamed the Canadian tundra. Today there are only about 7,000.

Circumpolar animals

Circumpolar animals are those that are found all around the world in the polar region—they circle the Pole. Caribou, reindeer, Arctic foxes and hares, wolves, lemmings, and human beings are circumpolar in the Arctic. The musk-ox was circumpolar, until it was hunted to extinction in Eurasia.

Ten thousand years ago there was a land bridge between Asia and America, where the Bering Strait now is. The animals moved from Siberia to America, probably to escape the colder temperatures and faster spread of ice in Asia. Only the wolf traveled the other way, from America to Eurasia.

The winter community

The tundra's climate is so harsh that few animals can stay all year. The herbivores feed on seeds and hay left from the summer's growth and on the thin winter plant life. The carnivores feed on the herbivores. A bad summer's growth may mean they all starve in winter.

Arctic wolf

Carnivores

The largest predator is the wolf, which hunts caribou, but will settle for carrion—the flesh of a dead animal. The Arctic fox hunts hares, lemmings, and voles and eats the wolf's leftovers, too. Weasels also eat lemmings, as does the snowy owl. The gyrfalcon eats small birds; the raven eats anything.

Arctic fox

Snowy owl

Gyrfalcon

Raven

Stoat

Herbivores

The lemming is the most common herbivore. Lemmings and voles live underground in summer and under the snow in winter. The Arctic hare roams aboveground. Plant-eating birds are the ptarmigan and the redpoll. The largest herbivore is the musk-ox.

Redpoll

Meadow vole

Ptarmigan

Lemming

Arctic hare

Musk-ox

11

Keeping out the cold

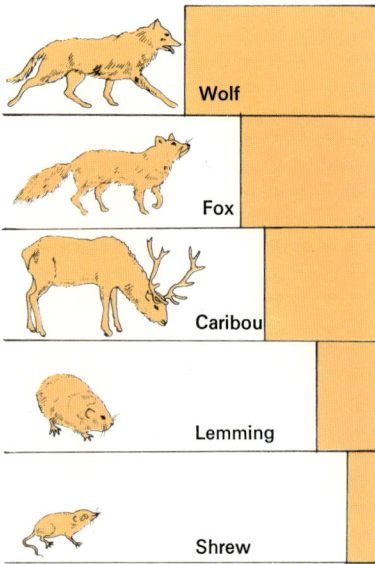

Thickness of fur

Tundra animals have thicker fur than animals of the same species in warmer areas. The thickness of the fur varies with the size of the animal. Wolves, foxes, and caribou have very thick pelts. Lemmings and shrews have thinner fur and spend winters under the snow.

Mammals and birds are the only warm-blooded animals. This means their bodies can keep up a fairly regular temperature in spite of their surroundings (cold-blooded animals take on the temperature of their surroundings). But in the Arctic there can be a difference of 150 degrees between an animal's blood temperature and the outside air. So the animals of the tundra have developed special characteristics to conserve, or save, their body heat.

Tundra animals are larger than similar animals in warmer climates. The larger an animal is, the more slowly it loses heat. Arctic animals also have more compact bodies. The parts of the body that stick out, the extremities (noses, ears, tails), lose heat into the air. In Arctic species, the extremities are smaller. The musk-ox has a thick neck and a short tail and legs. Birds have shorter legs and bills. Some animals can live with lower blood temperatures in their extremities. A reindeer's legs may be 50 degrees colder than its body.

The best way to stop heat loss is by insulation—a layer or cover of a material that holds in heat. Many animals have a layer of fat underneath the skin that serves both as insulation and a food reserve in winter. They have insulation outside the skin too: fur or feathers that trap warm air. Snowy owls and ptarmigans even have feathers on their toes. Caribou have heavy coats of air-filled hair.

Keeping warm

Heat is lost in two ways: by radiation where the heat moves in waves out into the air; and by conduction, where the heat is led or conducted away from the body by touching something else.

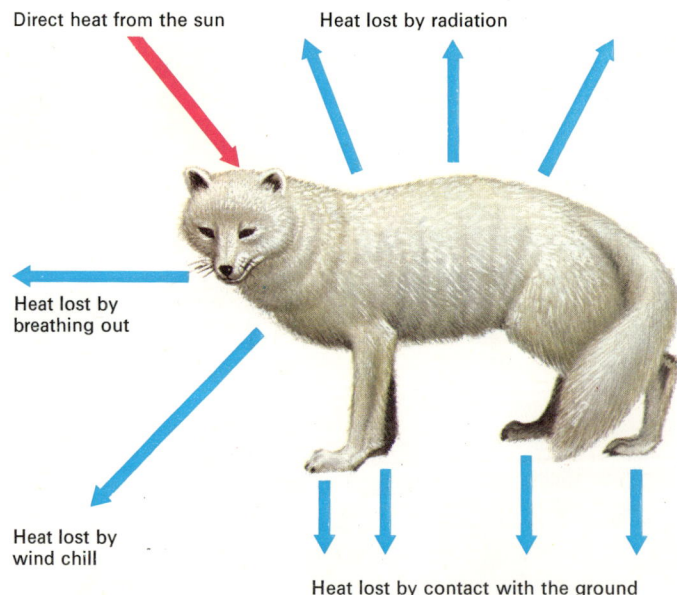

Direct heat from the sun

Heat lost by radiation

Heat lost by breathing out

Heat lost by wind chill

Heat lost by contact with the ground

Walking on the snow

Tundra animals have large, square feet that spread their weight over the surface of the snow so that they won't sink. Their feet are often covered with fur or feathers.

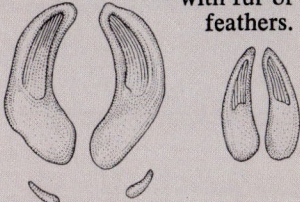

Caribou   Fallow deer

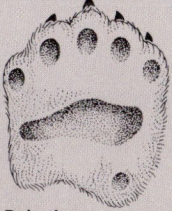   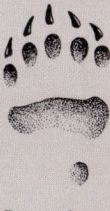

Polar bear   Brown bear

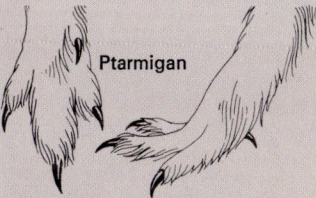

Ptarmigan

(from below)

A tundra resident

The musk-ox is the perfect tundra animal. It has a large, compact body, short legs and tail, and thick fur. It uses its huge feet to paw through the snow to reach the twigs and grass below.

Adapting to the climate

The parts of the animal's body that stick out lose at lot of heat. The fennec fox, a desert animal, has large ears and a long snout to lose heat quickly. The Arctic fox has small ears and an almost flat face to reduce heat loss. The red fox of the temperate zone has medium ears and snout because it doesn't live in an extreme climate. The desert jackrabbit has huge ears and a large snout, the Arctic hare has small, rounded ears, and the temperate hare comes in between.

Fennec fox

Red fox

Arctic fox

Jack rabbit

Hare

Arctic hare

The spring arrivals

In April the dark silence of the tundra winter is brightened by the cheerful song of the snow bunting. The ground is still snow-covered; no insects stir and no flowers lift their leaves. The sun makes only short daily appearances in some areas. But the arrival of this small bird means spring is on the way. In the next weeks millions of birds will return to their Arctic breeding grounds.

Around 100 species of birds spend the summer on the tundra, but only 6 are songbirds: the Lapland longspur, the wheatear, two kinds of pipits, and two sparrows. There are no trees for them to perch in and sing out their mating calls and claims to territory. So they perform song-flights instead, and sing while dancing through the air.

Most of the summer birds are waterfowl. They arrive in May, the peak of the migration season. Snow still blankets

Trumpeter swans

○ North America
□ Tundra regions
△ Siberia
◇ Northern Europe
▽ The Orient
● The Arctic
■ Subarctic
▲ Africa
◆ Eurasia

◇ Barnacle goose

●◆ Arctic loon

winter plumage

◇□● Lesser scaup

◆ Bear goose

△ Red breasted goose

○□ Common loon

△ Knot

○ Sandhill crane

● King eider duck

the land and the ponds are frozen. But the birds must mate early, so they can raise their young before the snow returns. Soon the whistling swans arrive and add new grass to their old nests. They mate for life and come back to the same place every year. When the ice breaks, ducks and loons fly in. In June the champion long-distance migrator, the Arctic tern, arrives, after flying about 11,000 miles from the Antarctic, where it spends the winter. Knots and ruddy turnstones are next, and the last arrival is usually the red phalarope, in mid-June.

The long Arctic days make up for the short summer. The birds can gather more food and so feed larger broods than similar birds living where days are shorter. The remoteness of the birds' nesting sites helps protect them from at least one enemy—egg-collecting human beings.

◇▽ Whooper swan

●■ Blue snow goose

◇▲ Rock pipit

○ Snow goose

◇▽ Bewick's swan

●■ Old squaw duck

◇ Northern phalarope

◇▲ Red phalarope

Caribou and reindeer

In the spring other travelers also return to the tundra: the caribou of North America and the reindeer of Europe and Asia. The two animals belong to the same species of deer; but the reindeer is no longer wild and migrates under the watchful eyes of herders. The caribou are larger. They stand about four feet high at the shoulder and weigh up to 350 pounds.

Caribou are well adapted to tundra life. They feed on lichens and grasses. Their huge feet support them on spongy ground or on snow and are good shovels for digging through the snow for food. Caribou can gallop up to 40 miles an hour and can swim when water blocks their migration paths. Both males and females have large, branching antlers. They shed them and grow new ones every year.

Caribou graze in small herds of less than a hundred. In the summer they like high ground where the wind gives them some relief from caribou flies. As fall approaches, the herds collect into large groups and begin their trek to winter feeding grounds south of the tundra. In the spring they return, bringing their calves, who are able to travel with the herd a few hours after birth.

In 1900 there were 25 million caribou in North America. Migrating herds were so big, it could take a week for one to pass a single spot. But hunters killed so many that today there are only about 600,000 in North America.

The large predators

Timber wolves
The timber, or gray, wolf lives almost everywhere in the Arctic, although in some areas the wolf has been hunted out of existence by human beings.

The best hunters of the tundra are wolves. These powerful carnivores weigh well over 100 pounds. They are social animals; they travel and hunt in organized packs of about twenty. One male leads and decides where to go and what to attack. If a leader is challenged by another wolf, he snarls and shows his fangs. The challenger usually rolls onto his back to uncover his throat (where he can be easily hurt), showing he accepts the leader. But if the leader is old or weak, the challenger might snarl back and a fight for leadership follows. Females struggle for position, too. Only the male and female leaders reproduce, so offspring are born to the strongest pack members.

Wolves eat up to twenty pounds of meat at a meal. They follow caribou all year, preying on the young, the old, and the sick. In areas where wolves have been wiped out by human beings, a caribou herd may be destroyed by disease, since there are no predators to kill off sick animals before the disease spreads.

The other large tundra predator is the grizzly bear. Bears are not as cunning as wolves and are not social animals. Males roam alone, and females travel only with their cubs. The grizzlies feed mostly on berries and plants but they also eat fish, insects, eggs, and ground squirrels. They are too slow for bigger game, but will feed on any dead animals they find.

Wolves
Wolves hunt in organized packs. If the prey puts up a strong battle, the wolf pack sometimes abandons the fight and looks for easier prey.

Wolverine

The wolverine is the largest member of the weasel family.

Lynx

The lynx is the only cat to visit the tundra in winter, in search of hares, voles, and lemmings.

Red fox

The red fox visits in summer, looking for birds and small animals.

Grizzly bear

It takes a grizzly eight to ten years to reach its full standing height of seven or eight feet. But the bear is not as fierce as it looks and will not usually attack large game unless it is already injured or dying. The grizzly lives in the tundra and mountain forests of western North America.

The season of plenty

Summer brings the tundra into full glory. As the snow melts in the June sunshine, the top few feet of soil thaw and water seeps down to the plant roots. The plants have been ready with buds that developed the previous summer, and now the flowers race into bloom. The saxifrage is usually the first, and others follow quickly.

Insects and other forms of tiny animal life emerge with the plants. Millions of caterpillars creep up grasses and twigs to feed above the melting snow. Ponds and lakes are crowded with mosquito larvae and other insect life. Spiders, plant lice, and beetles appear, and springtails—tiny insects that jump by pushing with their tails—are everywhere. A square

1. Ground squirrel
2. Sandhill crane
3. Whistling swans
4. Arctic fox
5. Spectacled eider duck
6. Red-breasted merganser
7. Old squaw duck
8. Musk-oxen
9. Caribou
10. Snow geese
11. Canada geese

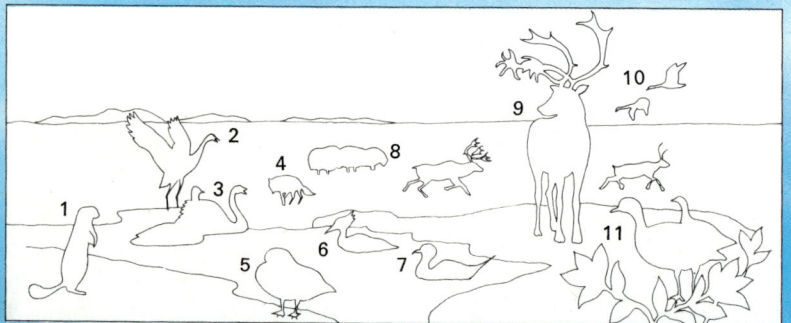

yard of plant life might hold a half million. The busy hum of bumblebees continues through the long day.

By July, duck and geese eggs are hatching, providing a feast for foxes, birds of prey, and even some fish. Snowy owls and ravens swoop down on lemmings, and weasels chase hares and ground squirrels. Everywhere creatures are eating and being eaten, for a banquet requires food as well as diners. Some animals, such as the fox, even store food for the winter.

In spite of the endless search for food, summer on the tundra can seem peaceful. Contented wolves, well-fed on small prey, sometimes walk among the grazing caribou and neither gives the other a second look.

The lemming year

As brave as a lemming
When cornered, lemmings will turn to fight, even though they are only about five inches long and no match for their predators. They have even been known to rush threateningly at human beings.

According to folklore, every few years millions of lemmings swarm to the water's edge and plunge in, only to drown. It is true that in some years hordes of these small rodents die—but not as suicides. The lemming population goes up and down in four-year cycles. It builds for three years to a boom, or "lemming" year. Then it crashes so low that lemmings are hard to find.

The cycle begins when good weather provides abundant food. The lemmings have extra litters—as many as eight a year instead of five or six. In spite of many predators, the population grows until there may be 1,000 for each original pair. The plant life can't support them, and so bands of lemmings go searching for food. This explains the stories of armies of moving lemmings.

The lemming boom leads to the crash. The huge population attracts more predators—foxes, owls, and others—from surrounding areas. In searching for food, some lemmings drown while trying to cross wide stretches of water, even though they swim well. The birthrate goes down too, because of overcrowding. By the next summer the population is down to one in 400, and the cycle begins again.

Other tundra animals have population cycles, some a result of the lemming boom. Owls and foxes produce more young in lemming years, since food is so easy to find. Ptarmigan have ten-year cycles and hares, too, have booms and crashes.

Lemmings
Two kinds of lemmings live on the tundra: brown lemmings and collared lemmings, who have a dark stripe on their backs and who become white in winter. Both live in underground tunnels.

A lemming predator

The snowy owl's eggs hatch two or three at a time. In a year when food is scarce, the first ones born may get enough to eat, but the owlets that hatch later may starve or be eaten by the older ones. In a lemming year, all the owlets survive.

Lemming explosions

The lemming population cycle lasts about four years, although it may be shorter or longer depending upon when the population peak is reached. Lemming booms (black line) are followed by increases in the populations of lemming predators (red line).

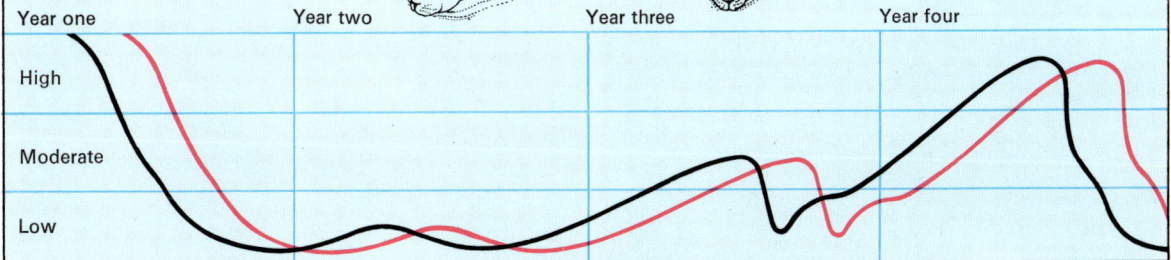

Year one	Year two	Year three	Year four

High

Moderate

Low

Migrating birds

Most of the birds who migrate south leave the tundra in July and August. The changing number of daylight hours may be their signal to leave.

Sleeping bears

Grizzly bears spend winter in a doze. They don't truly hibernate, for while their heartbeats and breathing slow, their temperature stays high. In January or February the females give birth to cubs, without really stirring from their dozing state.

The end of summer

In August the tundra offers the last course of its summer feast—a generous serving of ripe berries. Birds and mammals, even meat-eating wolves and foxes, stuff themselves with cloudberries, bilberries, and crowberries.

Plants finish their summer growth and produce buds that will blossom the next spring. Some start to dry out so they will not freeze. On the bottoms of ponds, gnat larvae and midges bury themselves in mud, to wait out the winter.

Hordes of migrating birds leave for warmer areas. Some adults left in July, but their chicks stayed to mature. Now the young birds flock together and leave for places they have never seen, guided by instinct. The caribou collect in groups for their walk south.

Many of the animals who stay all year change to white coats to hide from predators. Grizzly bears find dens for their long winter naps, and the tundra's only true hibernator, the ground squirrel, is already in its nest.

Ground squirrels

The ground squirrel is the only tundra animal that hibernates. They spend the winter in a sleep-like state: their breathing rate slows down and their heartbeat drops from 200 beats a minute to less than 10. From August until May they stay in grass-lined nests, dug deep into banks. The entrance is lower than the nest itself, so that warm air is trapped inside.

Winter coats

Some of the tundra animals shed their coats in August and grow white coats for winter. The white coats help keep out the cold since the hairs, which in summer contain color, now hold air instead.

Weasel

Arctic hare

Ptarmigan

Arctic fox

The long night

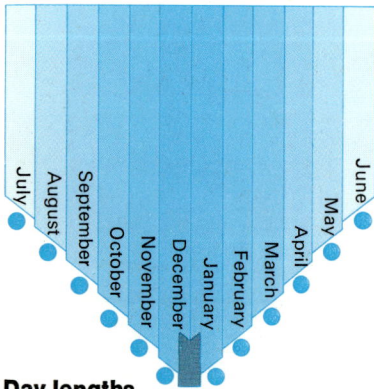

In winter, much of the tundra gets no sun for weeks. Since no snow melts, the land is blanketed with white. A few shrubs poke branches above the snow and provide food for the ptarmigan and some others. Musk-oxen in thick winter coats move to high exposed ground where the winds blow the snow from the grasses they feed on. The foxes eat the food they stored away during the summer. Arctic hares in white pelts are almost invisible against the snow as they roam about in large groups, looking for frozen plants to chew on.

On the surface, the tundra is a dark, cold, and quiet world. But underneath the snow there is more going on. Here it may be 40 degrees warmer than at the surface, and the temperature stays at about the same level—25 degrees, a little below freezing. The snow is a blanket of insulation; it protects the ground from cold wind and holds in the

Day lengths

In the Arctic, the nights are very short in June and July, the height of the summer. But after August, the number of daylight hours goes down very quickly and for eight months the Arctic is dark and gloomy.

Above and below

Arctic hares, musk-oxen, and wolves search for food above the snow. Foxes can dig into it. Ermine and other weasels hunt lemmings and voles in their tunnels under the snow.

warmth that the earth radiates or sends out from its deepest level. The steady heat from the hot center of the earth makes the snow next to the ground evaporate—it is warmed and turns into water vapor. This clears an air space between the earth and the snow.

In this space under the snow, small animals like shrews, voles, and lemmings spend the winter. They are too small to survive the cold above, but in this space they can keep warm enough to live. The winter is like summer for these animals—except that it is always dark under the snow. The plant eaters can find vegetation and the shrews eat the larvae and insects that are lying dormant. The dangers they meet are like the summer ones, too. Weasels—called ermine when they are in their white winter coats—are thin and flexible enough to move around under the snow to hunt for voles and lemmings.

Hoary Redpoll
The redpoll lives in the high regions of Greenland. It has an extra crop, or stomach, where it stores seeds to eat through the long night.

The warm snow blanket
The temperature below the snow stays at about the same level—27 degrees. As the snow next to the ground evaporates, it turns directly into vapor without going through a liquid stage. The water vapor rises to the snow where it refreezes, leaving an air space between the snow and the ground.

0° F

3° F

27° F

The caribou Eskimos

People have found ways to live almost everywhere on earth, including the tundra. Like other tundra animals, they are circumpolar. There are Eskimos on the American tundra, Lapps in northern Europe, Koryaks, Yakuts, and Samoyeds in Siberia. Nearly all these people depend on caribou, or their tame cousins, the reindeer. This species of deer may have first led people to the Arctic. The animals followed the shrinking ice caps north, and people followed the animals—their food source. In Eurasia, the people migrated with a herd, began to feel they owned it, and started to protect it from other predators, like wolves. This led to today's reindeer and reindeer economy.

The caribou in North America are hunted, not herded. In summer, Eskimos come inland to the trails caribou use in migrating from the tundra to the forest. Before they had rifles, they attacked swimming caribou with spears from their boats. Now, except for the shortage of caribou, hunting is easy. The beasts are nearsighted, so hunters raise their arms like antlers and walk within shooting range. All of the animal is used: meat and skins for food and clothing, fatty tallow for lamps, and even bone marrow as a kind of chewing gum.

Caribou Eskimos

The caribou Eskimos depend on the caribou for their living. They eat the meat and cure the skins—scraping them clean and hanging them to dry. The skins are used for tents, clothing, and sleeping rugs. The caribou hairs are air-filled and so the skins float. An Eskimo family can wrap belongings in a skin and then float it across a body of water.

Lapps

The Lapps were once completely dependent on animals. Armed with spears or harpoons, they hunted seal, caribou, and wolverines. The meat was eaten or dried and stored. The skin was cured and used for tents, bedding, and clothing. The bones were carved into tools. Even the intestines were used—scraped thin for windows.

Once the caribou were domesticated (and then called reindeer), they were used as pack animals and as a source for milk and cheese. Today, the life of the Lapps is more like that of other Scandinavian peoples.

Caribou

Ringed seal

Wolverine

Harpoon

Skin-scraping tools

The last wilderness

The Arctic tundra is the last great living wilderness on the land surface of the earth. It seems sure that it will not stay this way. For thousands of years, civilization has been creeping north. In the jet age, the Arctic Ocean is the new Mediterranean—the shortest way from almost anywhere to almost everywhere. Air bases and radar stations line the tundra's shores. Since industry has found that the Arctic is rich in copper, gold, nickel, and, above all, oil, the advance of civilization has speeded up.

Parks and game reserves have been established around the Pole, but the wild tundra is not likely to survive. Its system of natural communities of interdependent plants and animals can be upset too easily. There are too few species of plants and animals. The land itself is easily hurt. The tundra is marked by the tires of trucks driven over the spongy ground. The tracks freeze and then collect water. Some have been there for years. They may remain for centuries.